CODING IS EVERYWHERE

Coding in Transportation

by Elizabeth Noll

BELLWETHER MEDIA • MINNEAPOLIS, MN

Note to Librarians, Teachers, and Parents:

Blastoff! Readers are carefully developed by literacy experts and combine standards-based content with developmentally appropriate text.

Level 1 provides the most support through repetition of high-frequency words, light text, predictable sentence patterns, and strong visual support.

Level 2 offers early readers a bit more challenge through varied simple sentences, increased text load, and less repetition of high-frequency words.

Level 3 advances early-fluent readers toward fluency through increased text and concept load, less reliance on visuals, longer sentences, and more literary language.

Level 4 builds reading stamina by providing more text per page, increased use of punctuation, greater variation in sentence patterns, and increasingly challenging vocabulary.

Level 5 encourages children to move from "learning to read" to "reading to learn" by providing even more text, varied writing styles, and less familiar topics.

Whichever book is right for your reader, Blastoff! Readers are the perfect books to build confidence and encourage a love of reading that will last a lifetime!

This edition first published in 2019 by Bellwether Media, Inc.

No part of this publication may be reproduced in whole or in part without written permission of the publisher. For information regarding permission, write to Bellwether Media, Inc., Attention: Permissions Department, 6012 Blue Circle Drive, Minnetonka, MN 55343.

Library of Congress Cataloging-in-Publication Data

LC record for Coding in Transportation available at https://lccn.loc.gov/2017060190

Editor: Christina Leaf   Designer: Brittany McIntosh

Printed in the United States of America, North Mankato, MN

Table of Contents

Coding in Transportation

Did you know there are computers in your car? Most cars use more than 24 computers!

Planes, ships, and other **vehicles** have computers, too.

plane
cockpit

5

Vehicles count on computers to work well. Computers help the engine and brakes run smoothly.

mechanic fixing brakes

They also control **interior** parts, like the heat and radio.

All the computers in a
vehicle use **code**.

Code is a set of instructions written in a **programming language**. It tells the computer what to do.

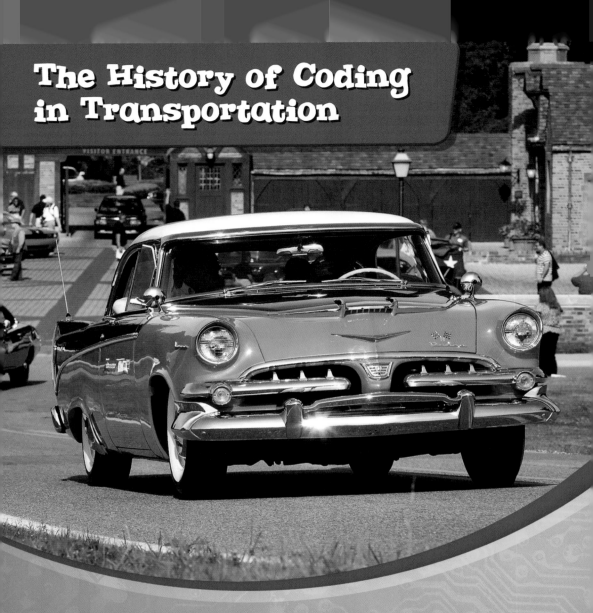

The History of Coding in Transportation

Before the late 1960s, cars had few **electronics** besides radios.

Carmakers first used simple computers to get better **gas mileage**.

Volkswagon Type III

11

Car **engineers** used more electronics in the 1980s and 1990s.

**1984
Dodge Omni GLH**

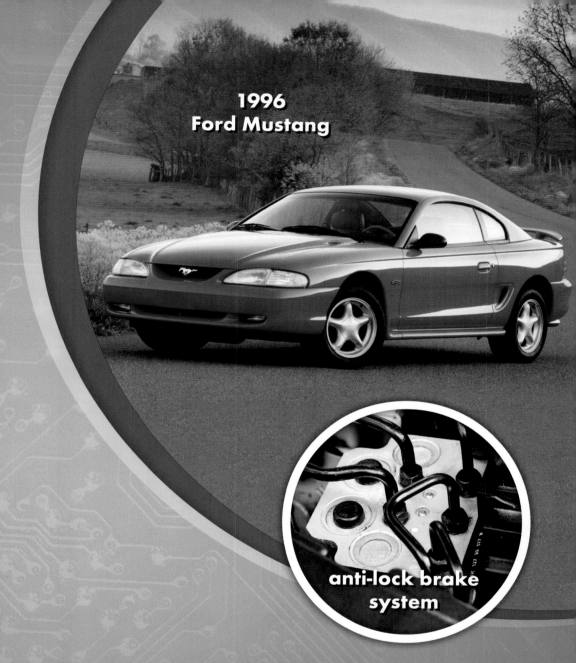

**1996
Ford Mustang**

anti-lock brake
system

Many were safety features.
These included air bags and
anti-lock brakes.

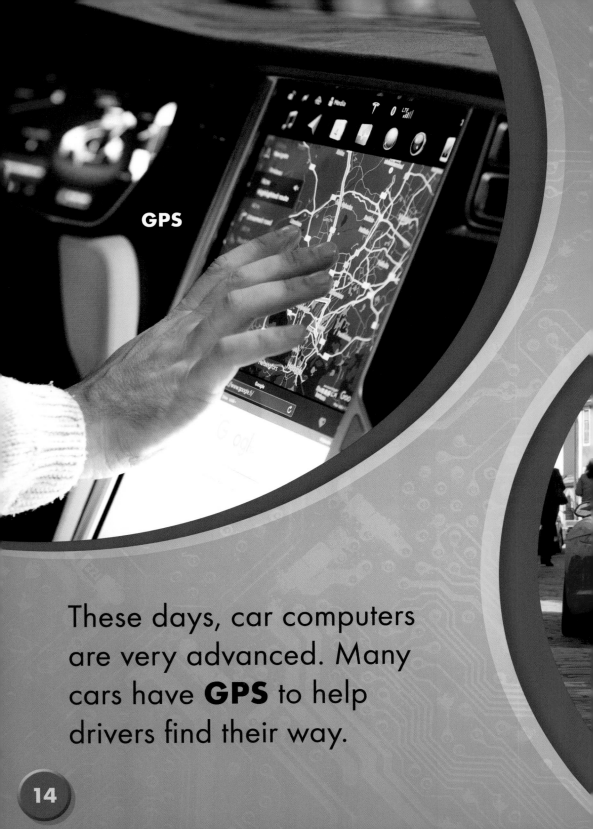

GPS

These days, car computers are very advanced. Many cars have **GPS** to help drivers find their way.

Some cars can park themselves!

Tesla Model S

How Does Coding Work in Transportation?

Sensors tell the car's computers what is happening. They measure light, speed, and other things.

backup camera

Check entire surroundings

sensors check car's surroundings

Tesla autopilot sensor

Code uses this information to direct the computers' actions.

For example, a driver brakes on ice and the car slips. Sensors warn the computer.

Code tells the computer to apply anti-lock brakes. The car stops!

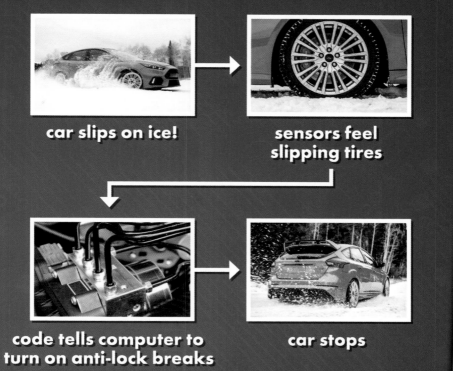

Anti-lock Brakes

car slips on ice!

sensors feel slipping tires

code tells computer to turn on anti-lock breaks

car stops

As cars have more
computers, they need more
code. Some cars today have
100 million lines of code.

What code would you write for a car?

Glossary

anti-lock brakes—a brake system that prevents the wheels from locking up so the driver can still steer

code—instructions for a computer

electronics—devices that use many small electrical parts in order to work; televisions, radios, and computers are common electronics.

engineers—people who work on machines or engines

gas mileage—the number of miles a car can go per gallon of gas

GPS—short for global positioning system; GPS tells people where they are and can give directions.

interior—the inside of a car

programming language—a special language that humans use to talk to computers

sensors—devices that respond to light, pressure, sound, or other physical changes

vehicles—machines that are used for carrying or transporting

To Learn More

AT THE LIBRARY

Hubbard, Ben. *How Coding Works*. Chicago, Ill.: Capstone, 2017.

Lyons, Heather. *Coding in the Real World*. Minneapolis, Minn.: Lerner Publications, 2018.

Wainewright, Max. *How to Code: A Step-by-Step Guide to Computer Coding*. New York, N.Y.: Sterling Publishing, 2016.

ON THE WEB

Learning more about coding in transportation is as easy as 1, 2, 3.

1. Go to www.factsurfer.com.

2. Enter "coding in transportation" into the search box.

3. Click the "Surf" button and you will see a list of related web sites.

With factsurfer.com, finding more information is just a click away.

Index

The images in this book are reproduced through the courtesy of: Ivan Kurmyshov, front cover; Chrysler, pp. 4, 10, 12; Skycolors, p. 5; navee sangvitoon, p. 6; kryzhov, p. 7; Leeloona, p. 8; Rolf Geithe, p. 9; Phil Talbot/Alamy, p. 11; The Ford Motor Company, pp. 13 (top), 18, 19 (top left, top right, bottom right), 20; Ensuper, p. 13 (bottom); Aleksandra Suzi, p. 14; chasdesign, p. 15; peych_p, p. 16; Tesla, p. 17 (all); APITHANA, p. 19 (bottom left); chombosan, p. 21.